Diabetic Cookbook

On a Budget

Beef Recipes

Great-tasting, Easy and Healthy Recipes for Every Day

Angela Moore

Table of Contents

Intruduction

If you have diabetes, watching what you eat is by far one of the most important ways of staying healthy. The goal should be to avoid spikes in your blood sugar (blood glucose levels). Some people interpret this as needing to completely avoid sugar and carbohydrates, which isn't entirely accurate. In fact, people typically need 40-60% of their calories to come from carbohydrates. It's the amount and consistency of carbohydrates in a diabetic diet that makes the biggest difference in controlling blood glucose levels.

As a diabetic, you can and should eat a wide variety of foods. So instead of focusing on eliminating certain foods from your diet, emphasize increasing vegetables and fruits, limiting added fats and sugars, and paying close attention to portion size. For example, it's probably okay to eat peaches, melons, and dried fruits if you are being carefully not to eat too much. These basic healthy eating practices are key, along with establishing a regular exercise routine. Establishing lasting healthy behaviors is much more important than focusing on how much weight you need to lose right now, and the foods you should eliminate from your diet.

What does the diet consist of?

The diabetic diet can vary from person to person depending on diagnosis, current nutritional status, blood glucose levels, glycated haemoglobin, blood lipids, and blood pressure. Regardless, it generally consists of monitoring the daily intake of macronutrients: carbohydrates, protein, and fat. Specifically, patients need to watch their carbohydrate intake because it is the main factor affecting postprandial blood glucose levels.

What are the nutritional recommendations of a diabetic diet?

The amount of carbohydrate in the diet is individualized based on the person's usual intake and desired glucose and lipid goals. Daily intake of carbohydrates can range from 45% to 60% of total calories. Blood glucose and insulin response are influenced by both the source and amount of carbohydrates consumed. Of the two, priority is given to the total amount of carbohydrate consumed at each meal and snack rather than the source of carbohydrate.

Protein intake should consist of 10% to 20% of the daily calories. Dietary protein can be obtained from vegetable and animal sources. Fat intake should be 25% to 30% of total calories for the day. It is important to keep track of your lipid levels with your doctor. Cholesterol should be limited to less than 300 mg a day.

1. Salsa Marinated Steak

Yield: 4 servings

Ingredients:

- 11/4 pounds (570 g) boneless beef chuck, cut 1-inch thick
- 1/3 cup (87 g) salsa, prepared,
- 2 tablespoons (30 ml) lime juice, fresh
- 1 garlic clove, minced
- 1 teaspoon oregano leaves, dried
- 1/4 teaspoon cumin, ground

Directions:

1. Combine salsa, lime juice, garlic, oregano, and cumin; reserve 2 tablespoons (30 ml) marinade.

2. Place beef steaks in plastic bag; add remaining marinade, turning to coat.
3. Close bag securely and marinate in refrigerator 6 to 8 hours (or overnight, if desired), turning occasionally.
4. Remove steaks from marinade and place on grill over medium coals.
5. Grill 18 to 24 minutes for rare to medium, turning once.
6. Brush with reserved marinade during last 5 minutes of cooking.
7. Carve into thin slices.

Nutritional Info:100 g water; 430 calories (58% from fat, 39% from protein, 2% from carb); 41 g Protein; 27 g total fat; 11 g saturated fat; 12 g monounsaturated fat; 1 g polyunsaturated fat; 2 g

2. Beef Hamburger

Serving: 4

Ingredients:

- 20 g 85% lean ground beef, cooked
- 20 g 40% heavy cream
- 21.2 g mayonnaise, Hellmann's TM
- 10 g European-style butter
- 10 g Kraft Cheddar cheese, block style, grated
- salt/pepper

Directions:

1. After measuring all ingredients on a gram scale, combine in a small nonstick skillet.

2. Heat on medium heat until the cheese is melted and all the ingredients have combined.
3. Do not overcook or bring to a boil, this will cause the sauce to "break" and the oil to separate.

3.Philly Cheesesteak Lettuce Cups

Serving: 4

Ingredients:

- 3 ounces lean beef steak
- 1/3 cup sliced mushrooms
- 1/4 cup tinly sliced onions
- 1 slice fat-free American cheese
- 2 leaves romaine, butter or green leaf lettuce

Directions

1. Slice meat into thin strips.
2. Coat medium pan with nonstick cooking spray.
3. Add mushrooms and onions; cook over medium heat for 5 minutes, stirring occasionally, until onions are slightly browned.
4. Set aside.
5. Remove pan from heat and re-coat with nonstick cooking spray.
6. Cook steak strips over medium heat for 1-2 minutes, flipping halfway through.
7. Break cheese slice into small strips.
8. Place cheese on top of meat--still in the pan-- and continue to cook until cheese melts.
9. Remove from heat; mix beef strips with veggies and serve on lettuce leaves.

Nutritional Facts

Calories 197 Protein 13.5 g Fat 7.5 g (3 g saturated)

Cholesterol 55 mg Carbohydrates 7 g Sodium 185 mg

Fiber 1 g Sugar: 4 g

4. Texas Style Steak

Yield: 6 servings

Ingredients:

- 1/2 cup (63 g) flour
- 21/2 teaspoons (6.5 g) chili powder, divided
- 11/2 pounds (680 g) beef round steak
- 2 tablespoons (30 ml) vegetable oil
- 1/2 cup (75 g) green peppers, chopped
- 1/2 cup (80 g) onions, chopped
- 1 cup (235 ml) fat-free beef broth
- 1/2 cup (120 ml) tomato juice
- 1/4 teaspoon garlic powder

- 1/4 teaspoon ground cumin

Directions:

1. Blend flour, salt, and 11/2 teaspoons (4 g) chili powder well and place in pie pan.
2. Dredge meat in the flour mixture.
3. Place oil in a heavy frying pan and heat over moderate heat.
4. Add meat and brown on both sides.
5. Transfer steaks to a 1112 quart (1.5 L) casserole.
6. Fry peppers and onions over moderate heat in the pan in which the meat was browned, stirring frequently. Remove vegetables with a slotted spoon and spread over meat.
7. Pour out any remaining fat. Add beef broth to frying pan and cook and stir over moderate heat to absorb and brown particles remaining in the pan.
8. Add remaining ingredients to broth.
9. Mix well and pour over meat. Stir the meat and vegetables lightly with a fork to distribute the broth and vegetables.
10. Cover tightly and bake at 325°F (170°C, or gas mark 3) for about 1-1112 hours or until the meat is tender.

Nutritional Info:149 g water; 322 calories (31 % from fat, 55% from protein, 14% from carb); 43 g Protein; 11 g total fat; 3 g

5. Low-Carb Beef Stroganoff

Servings: 4

Ingredients:

- 1 1/2 lb beef tenderloin -- thin strips
- 2 tbsp all-purpose flour
- 2 tbsp butter

- 2 tbsp olive oil
- 1 1/2 cups beef bouillon
- 1/4 cup sour cream
- 2 tbsp tomato paste
- 1/2 tsp paprika
- salt to taste

Directions

1. Dredge beef in flour.
2. In a heavy skillet, melt butter with oil.
3. Brown the beef (about 5 minutes).
4. Slowly add bouillon to beef, stirring well.
5. Bring to a boil.
6. Combine sour cream, tomato paste, paprika, and salt. Slowly stir sour cream mixture into beef mixture.
7. Turn heat to low and bring to a bare simmer. Cook 15-20 minutes, stirring frequently and never allowing mixture to boil.

6.Indian Red Curry

Servings: 4

Ingredients:

- 1 lb beef stew
- 1 tbsp butter
- 1/2 tsp curry paste -- or powder
- 1 dash cinnamon,cardamom, and pepper
- 1 cup canned coconut milk
- 1/2 cup red pepper
- 1 tsp paprika
- 1 garlic clove

Directions

1. Brown meat and garlic in butter, then add spices and stir fry few minutes.
2. Add red pepper and coconut milk.
3. Reduce heat and simmer til done (2-3 hours, add water if necessary.)

7. Corned Beef and Cabbage

Servings: 6

Ingredients:

- 4 cups Hot Water
- 2 tbsp Cider Vinegar
- 2 tbsp Splenda
- 1/2 tsp Pepper -- Freshly Ground
- 1 Large Onion -- Cut Into Wedges
- 3 lb Corned Beef -- 1.5kg With Spices
- 1 Cabbage

- Cored And Cut into 10 Wedges

Directions

1. In a 6 quart – 6 litre crock pot, combine the water, vinegar, splenda, pepper, and onions, mixing well.
2. Place the corned beef into the mixture.
3. Cover and cook on high heat for 4 hours.
4. Remove the lid and scatter the cabbage wedges over the top.
5. Cover and continue cooking on high 3 to 4 hours longer, or until the beef is tender.
6. To serve, carve the beef into slices and serve with the cabbage, with some of the cooking liquid spooned over the beef to keep it moist.

Nutritional Facts

248 Calories 20g Fat (70.5% calories from fat)

9g Protein 10g Carbohydrate 2g Dietary Fiber

35mg Cholesterol 522mg Sodium

8.   Barbecue Meat Loaf

Yield: 6 servings

Ingredients:

- 1/4 cup (40 g) onion, finely chopped
- 1/4 cup (25 g) celery, finely chopped
- 1/4 cup (60 g) low-sodium catsup
- 1 egg
- 1/4 cup (30 g) dry bread crumbs
- 1 teaspoon (5 ml) liquid smoke
- Dash black pepper
- 11/2 pounds (680 g) lean ground beef

Directions:

1. Place all ingredients except beef in mixing bowl and mix well.
2. Add beef to catsup mixture and mix until blended.
3. Shape into a loaf about 3112 x 7-inch (9 x 18 cm).
4. Place in a pan that has been sprayed with nonstick vegetable oil spray or lined with aluminum foil.
5. Bake at 325°F (170°C, or gas mark 3) about 1 hour or until browned and firm.
6. Pour off any fat and drippings and let set for 10 minutes before cutting into 6 equal slices.

Nutritional Info:94 g water; 311 calories (61 % from fat, 30% from protein, 9% from carb); 23 g Protein; 21 g total fat; 8 g

9.Home-Style Meat Loaf

Yield: 6 servings

Ingredients:

- 3/4 cup (180 g) ketchup, divided
- 1/2 cup (40 g) quick-cooking oats
- 1/4 cup (40 g) minced onion
- 2 tablespoons (8 g) chopped parsley
- 1 tablespoon (1 5 g) brown sugar
- 1/4 teaspoon black pepper
- 2 large egg whites, lightly beaten
- 11/2 pounds (680 g) ground round

Directions:

1. Preheat oven to 350°F (180°C, gas mark 4).
2. Combine 112 cup (120 g) ketchup, oats, and next 6 ingredients (oats through egg whites) in a large bowl.
3. Add meat; stir just until blended.
4. Shape meat mixture into an 8 x 4-inch (20 x 10 cm) loaf on a broiler pan coated with nonstick vegetable oil spray.
5. Brush remaining ketchup over meat loaf. Bake 11/2 hours or until done.

Nutritional Info:110 g water; 363 calories (51 % from fat, 28% from protein, 21 % from carb); 25 g protein; 20 g total fat; 8 g

10. German Meatballs

Yield: 6 servings

Ingredients:

- 1 egg
- 1/4 cup (60 ml) skim milk
- 1/4 cup (30 g) bread crumbs
- 1/4 teaspoon poultry seasoning
- 1 pound (455 g) extra-lean ground beef
- 2 cups (475 ml) low-sodium beef broth
- 1/2 cup (35 g) sliced mushrooms
- 1/2 cup (80 g) chopped onion
- 1 cup (230 g) fat-free sour cream
- 1 tablespoon (8 g) flour
- 1 teaspoon caraway seed

Directions:

1. Combine egg and milk.
2. Stir in crumbs and seasoning.
3. Add meat and mix well.
4. Form into 24 meatballs, about 11/2 inches (31/2 cm).
5. Brown meatballs in skillet.
6. Drain. Add broth, mushrooms, and onion. Cover and simmer for 30 minutes.
7. Stir together sour cream, flour, and caraway seed. Stir into skillet.
8. Cook and stir until thickened.

Nutritional Info:194 g water; 281 calories (32% from fat, 47% from protein, 21 % from carb); 19 g protein; 6 g total fat; 2 g

11. Steak Plus

Yield: 4 servings

Ingredients:

- 11/2 pounds (680 g) beefsteak
- 1 clove garlic, cut in half
- 2 teaspoons black peppercorns, crushed
- 1/4 cup (55 g) unsalted butter
- 1 tablespoon (11 g) Dijon mustard
- 2 teaspoons Worcestershire sauce
- 1/2 teaspoon lime juice

Directions:

1. Trim fat on beefsteaks to 1/4-inch (112 cm) thickness. Rub garlic on beef.
2. Press peppercorns into beef.
3. Mix together the butter, mustard, Worcestershire sauce, and lime juice. Heat coals or gas grill.
4. Apply sauce to steak; cover and grill beef 4 to 5 inches (10 to 13 cm) from medium heat.
5. Turn steaks and apply sauce again; cook until desired doneness.

Nutritional Info:115 g water; 437 calories (52% from fat, 46% from protein, 2% from carb); 50 g protein; 25 g total fat;

12.   Sirloin Steak strips

Servings 6

Ingredients:

- 2 lb Beef, top sirloin steak, lean, raw
- 1 pinch salt and pepper (to taste)
- 1 tsp minced garlic
- 1/2 cup red wine (dry)
- 1/2 cup fat free unsalted beef broth
- 2 tbsp dijon mustard
- 3 tbsp chopped parsley

Directions

1. Cut the steak into strips about 3/4 inch thick, and heat a large skillet coated with nonstick cooking spray over medium high heat.
2. Sauté the steak on both sides until it is done, about 5 to 7 minutes, and season with the salt and pepper.
3. Remove the meat, and add the garlic and wine to the pan, and boil until reduced by half, stirring well, and add the beef broth and mustard,

stirring until blended. Boil until slightly thickened, and add the parsley, and return the meat to the pan,

Nutritional Facts

Amount Per Serving Calories 239.1 Total Carbs 1.8g

Dietary Fiber 0.1g Sugars 0.1g Total Fat 10.8g

Saturated Fat 4g Unsaturated Fat 6.8g Potassium

13.   Meatballs Arrabbiata

Servings: 6

Ingredients:

- 1/2 pound (225 g) Italian sausage

- 1/2 pound (225 g) lean ground beef

- 2 tablespoons (18 g) garlic powder

- 1 tablespoon (18 g) salt
- 1/2 cup (60 g) green pepper, seeded, cut in thin strips
- 1/2 cup (80 g) coarsely chopped onion
- 1 14-ounce (400 g) can diced tomatoes, with juice
- 1/2 cup (120 ml) chicken stock or water
- 2 tablespoons (12 g) crushed red pepper, or to taste

Directions:

1. Combine the Italian sausage and ground beef in a bowl. Add the garlic powder and salt.
2. Mix well
3. and roll into meatballs.
4. In a large skillet, brown the meatballs over medium heat.
5. After meatballs are browned allover (about 5 to 7 minutes), add remaining ingredients, stirring well.
6. Cover and simmer 15 minutes.

14.　Lean Sloppy Joe Filling

Serves 4; Serving Size: 1/2 recipe

Ingredients:

1 tablespoon olive oil

8 ounces lean ground beef

1/2 cup chopped white onion

1/2 cup chopped red bell pepper

1/2 cup shredded carrot

1 1/2 cups low-sodium tomato sauce

1/2 teaspoon chili powder

1 teaspoon paprika

1/2 teaspoon red pepper flakes

Directions:

1. Coat a medium-sized pan with the olive oil, add the meat, and brown for about 5–7 minutes, stirring frequently.
2. Remove meat from pan and set aside.

3. To the same pan, add the onions, bell peppers, and carrots and sauté on high heat until softened, about 6–7 minutes.

4. Add the tomato sauce, browned meat, and spices;

5. mix well and continue to cook, stirring occasionally until warmed through, about 5–8 minutes.

Nutritional Analysis (per serving):

Calories: 150 Protein: 13g Carbohydrates: 12g

Fat: 6g Saturated Fat: 1.5g Cholesterol: 30mg

Sodium: 70mg Fiber: 2g

15. Snappy Stuffed Peppers

Serves 4; Serving Size: 1 pepper

Ingredients:

- 4 bell peppers
- 1 tablespoon olive oil
- 1/2 pound extra-lean ground beef
- 7 ounces crushed tomatoes
- 1 cup chopped mushrooms
- 1/2 cup chopped white onion
- 1 teaspoon crushed garlic or 2 cloves chopped

- 1 1/2 teaspoons paprika
- 1 1/2 teaspoons ground cumin
- 1/2 cup corn (fresh, canned, or frozen thawed)
- 1/2 cup cooked brown rice
- 2 tablespoons chopped fresh cilantro
- 1/2 teaspoon salt
- 1/2 cup shredded low-fat cheese

Directions:

1. Preheat oven to 350°F. Cut the tops of the peppers off, hollow out, remove seeds, and set aside. Cook the peppers until soft but still firm/maintaining their shape: Place them in a pot of boiling water or microwave them in a 4-quart Pyrex dish filled with

1/2 l of water for about four minutes. Drain and set cooked peppers aside.

2. Coat a medium-sized pan with the olive oil, add the beef, and brown it for 5 minutes, stirring frequently.

3. Add the crushed tomatoes, mushrooms, onion, garlic, paprika, and cumin; mix well and continue to cook, stirring occasionally for about 5–8 minutes.

4. Once the mixture is mostly cooked and the beef is well browned, mix in the corn, rice, cilantro, and salt and cook for another 1–2 minutes.

5. Divide and add the mixture to the four cooked peppers.

6. Cover the dish with the lid or aluminum foil and bake for 35 minutes. Uncover, sprinkle with cheese, and bake for another few minutes until slightly melted.

Nutritional Analysis (per serving):

Calories: 260 Protein: 19g Carbohydrates: 26g Fat: 10g Saturated Fat: 3g Cholesterol: 40mg Sodium: 380mg Fiber: 5g

16.   Stovetop Grilled Beef Loin

Yields 1 (5-ounce) loin; Serving Size: 2 1/2 ounces

Ingredients:

- 1 lean beef tenderloin fillet, no more than 1" thick
- 1/2 teaspoon paprika
- 1 1/2 teaspoons garlic powder
- 1/2 teaspoon cracked black pepper
- 1/2 teaspoon onion powder
- Pinch to 1/2 teaspoon ground cayenne pepper (according to taste)
- 1/2 teaspoon dried oregano
- 1/2 teaspoon dried thyme
- 1/2 teaspoon brown sugar
- 1/2 teaspoon olive oil

Directions:

1. Remove loin from refrigerator 30 minutes before preparing it to allow it to come to room temperature. Pat meat dry with paper towels.

2. Mix together all dry ingredients. Rub 1/2 teaspoon of olive oil on each side of the fillet. (The olive oil is used in this recipe to help the "rub" adhere to the meat and to

aid in the caramelization process.) Divide seasoning mixture; rub into each oiled side.

3. Heat a grill pan on high for 1–2 minutes until the pan is sizzling hot. Place beef fillet in pan, reduce heat to medium-high, and cook 3 minutes. Use tongs to turn fillet. (Be careful not to pierce meat.) Cook for another 2 minutes for medium or 3 minutes for well-done.

4. Remove from heat and let the meat rest in pan for at least 5 minutes, allowing juices to redistribute throughout meat and complete cooking process, which makes for a juicier fillet.

5.Weights and Measures: Before and After Exchanges are based on cooking weights of meats; however, in the case of lean pork loin trimmed of all fat, very little weight is lost during the cooking process.

6.Therefore, amounts given for raw pork loin in recipes equal cooked weights. If you find your cooking method causes more variation in weight, adjust accordingly.

Nutritional Analysis (per serving):

Calories: 105 Protein: 15g Carbohydrates: 1g Fat: 4g

Saturated Fat: 1g Cholesterol: 2mg Sodium: 27mg

17. Grilled Cheeseburger Sandwich

Serves 4; Serving Size: 1/2 sandwich

Ingredients:

- 1 tablespoon olive oil
- 1 teaspoon butter
- 2 thick slices 7-Grain Bread (see recipe in Chapter 2)
- 1-ounce Cheddar cheese slice
- 1/2 pound (8 ounces) ground round
- 1 teaspoon Worcestershire sauce or to taste
- Fresh minced garlic to taste
- Balsamic vinegar to taste

Directions:

1. Preheat indoor grill.
2. Combine olive oil and butter; use half to butter one side of each slice of bread.

3. Place Cheddar cheese on unbuttered side of one slice of bread; top with other slice of bread, buttered-side up.

4. Combine ground round with Worcestershire sauce, garlic, and balsamic vinegar if using.

5. Shape ground round into large, rectangular patty, a little larger than slice of bread.

6. Grill patty and then cheese sandwich. (If you are using a large indoor grill, position hamburger at lower end, near area where fat drains; grill cheese sandwich at

7. higher end.)

8. Once cheese sandwich is done, separate slices of bread, being careful not to burn yourself on cheese.

9. Top one side with hamburger and add your choice of condiments and fixings.

Nutritional Analysis (per serving):

Calories: 262 Protein: 17g Carbohydrates: 15g

Fat: 15g Saturated Fat: 5g Cholesterol: 60mg Sodium: 252mgFiber: 1.22g

18. Southwest Black Bean Burgers

Serves 5; Serving Size: 1 patty

Ingredients:

- 1 cup cooked black beans
- 1/2 cup chopped onion
- 1 teaspoon chili powder
- 1 teaspoon ground cumin
- 1 tablespoon minced fresh parsley
- 1 tablespoon minced fresh cilantro
- 1/2 teaspoon salt (optional)
- 1/2 pound lean ground beef

Directions:

1. Place beans, onion, chili powder, cumin, parsley, cilantro, and salt in food processor.

2. Combine ingredients using pulse setting until beans are partially puréed and all ingredients are mixed. (If using canned beans, drain and rinse first.)

3. In a separate bowl, combine ground beef and bean mixture. Shape into five patties.

4. Meat mixture is quite soft after mixing and should be chilled or partially frozen prior to cooking.

5. Grill or broil on oiled surface.

Nutritional Analysis (per serving):

Calories: 230 Protein: 20g Carbohydrates: 10g

Fat: 12g Saturated Fat: 4g Cholesterol: 55mg

Sodium: 15.02mg Fiber: 4g

19. Marinated London Broil

Yield: 6 servings

Ingredients:

- 11/2 pounds (680 g) flank steak or bottom round
- 1/4 cup (40 g) onion, finely chopped
- 1/3 cup (80 ml) Worcestershire sauce
- 2/3 cup (30 ml) dry red wine
- 2 tablespoons olive oil
- 1 teaspoon thyme

Directions:

1. With sharp knife, score steak on both sides.
2. In shallow platter or plastic bag, combine onion, Worcestershire sauce, wine, oil, and thyme.
3. Lay steak flat in marinade and turn to coat both
4. sides thoroughly.
5. Let stand for 30 minutes, turning occasionally.
6. Prepare and heat grill.
7. Grill about 5 minutes for first side and 4 minutes for second side, basting with marinade. To serve, cut crosswise in thin slanted slices.
8. Heat remaining marinade to boiling and spoon over slices.

Nutritional Info:105 g water; 296 calories (47% from fat, 48% from protein, 6% from carb); 32 g Protein; 14 g total fat; 5 g

20.   Texas Barbecued Steak

Yield: 4 servings

Ingredients:

- 4 sirloin steaks, 4 ounces (115 g) each
- 1/4 cup (85 g) honey
- 4 garlic cloves minced
- 2 teaspoons (4 g) black pepper, fresh ground
- 2 teaspoons (6 g) dry mustard
- 2 teaspoons (5.2 g) chili powder

Directions:

1. Rub each steak with 1 tablespoon honey. Combine remaining ingredients and rub onto steaks. Let stand 20 to 30 minutes.
2. Barbecue or broil to desired degree of doneness.

Nutritional Info:82 g water; 457 calories (50% from fat, 33% from protein, 17% from carb); 38 g Protein; 25 g total fat; 10 g sugar; 282

21. Soy and Ginger Flank Steak

Yield: 4 servings

Ingredients:

- 1 flank steak (11/4 pounds or 570 g)
- 1 tablespoon (6 g) minced fresh ginger
- 2 teaspoons minced garlic
- 1/4 cup (60 ml) Dick's Reduced-Sodium Soy Sauce (see chapter 2)
- 3 tablespoons (45 ml) dry red wine
- 11/2 tablespoons (30 g) honey

Directions:

1. Rinse the meat and pat dry.
2. Place steak in a plastic freezer bag (1-gallon size) and add the remaining ingredients; seal bag and turn to coat.
3. Lightly oil a barbecue grill and preheat to very hot.
4. Remove the steak from the bag, reserving marinade for vegetables (see note).
5. Cook steak, turning once until done as you like it (about 15 minutes total for medium-rare).
6. To serve, slice diagonally across the grain into thin slices.

Nutritional Info:115 g water; 320 calories (35% from fat, 53% from protein, 12% from carb); 40 g protein; 12 g total fat; 5 g

22. Oriental-Style Flank Steak

Yield: 4 servings

Ingredients:

- 11/2 pounds (680 g) flank steak
- 1/4 cup (25 g) sliced green onion
- 2 tablespoons (16 g) sesame seeds, toasted
- 1/2 cup (125 g) barbecue sauce
- 1 clove garlic, minced
- 1/4 cup (60 ml) Dick's Reduced-Sodium Soy Sauce (see chapter 2)
- 1/4 teaspoon ground ginger

Directions:

1. Score steak on both sides.
2. Pour combined ingredients over steak.
3. Cover; marinate in refrigerator several hours or overnight, turning once.
4. Place steak on rack of broiler pan.
5. Broil 15 to 20 minutes or until desired doneness, brushing frequently with barbecue sauce mixture and turning occasionally.

6. To serve, carve steak across grain with slanted knife into thin slices.

Nutritional Info:134 g water; 395 calories (34% from fat, 50% from protein, 16% from carb); 48 g protein; 14 g total fat; 6 g

23.   Deviled Steak

Yield: 6 servings

Ingredients:

- 2 pounds (900 g) beef round steak
- 2 tablespoons (30 ml) olive oil
- 3 tablespoons (30 g) minced onion
- 3/4 cup (180 g) low-sodium catsup
- 3/4 cup (175 ml) water
- 1/2 cup (120 ml) cider vinegar
- 1 tablespoon (15 g) brown sugar
- 1 tablespoon (11 g) prepared mustard
- 1 tablespoon (15 ml) Worcestershire sauce

Directions:

1. Cut meat into serving pieces.
2. In skillet, brown meat in oil over medium heat.
3. Remove meat to Dutch oven.
4. Add remaining ingredients to skillet. Simmer 5 minutes.
5. Pour mixture over meat.
6. Cover and bake 2 hours or until meat is tender.

Nutritional Info:159 g water; 396 calories (29% from fat, 58% from protein, 13% from carb); 56 g Protein; 12 g total fat; 3 g

24. Bourbon Barbecue-Sauced Beef Ribs

Yield: 6 servings

Ingredients:

- 3 pounds (11/3 kg) beef ribs

- 1/2 cup (120 ml) Jack Daniel's whiskey

- 1/4 cup (60 g) brown sugar

- 1/2 cup (120 g) low-sodium ketchup

- 1 teaspoon Worcestershire sauce

- 1 tablespoon (15 ml) vinegar

- 2 teaspoons lemon juice

- 1/2 teaspoon garlic powder

- 1/2 teaspoon dry mustard

Directions:

1. Precook ribs 1 hour in oven heated to 350°F (180°C, gas mark 4).
2. Meanwhile, preheat grill.
3. Combine sauce ingredients.
4. Transfer ribs to grill.
5. Brush with sauce. Baste and turn until done and crisp on the outside, about 30 minutes.

Nutritional Info:187 g water; 466 calories (42% from fat, 44% from protein, 14% from carb); 45 g protein; 19 g total fat; 8 g

25.   Braised Short Ribs

Yield: 6 servings

Ingredients:

- 4 pounds (1.8 kg) beef short ribs
- 1/2 cup (63 g) flour
- 11/2 teaspoons paprika
- 1/2 teaspoon dry mustard
- 11/2 cups (240 g) onion, sliced and separated into rings
- 1 clove garlic, chopped
- 1 cup (235 ml) beer or beef broth

Directions:

1. Place short ribs in skillet and brown to remove fat; drain well.
2. Combine flour with the paprika and dry mustard; toss with short ribs.
3. Place in slow cooker.
4. Place remaining ingredients over beef.
5. Cook on low for 8-10 hours.

Nutritional Info:283 g water; 596 calories (49% from fat, 42% from protein, 9% from carb); 59 g Protein; 31 g total fat; 13

26. Spinach and Mushroom-Stuffed Tenderloin

Yield: 10 servings

Ingredients:

- 4 tablespoons (55 g) butter (or margarine)
- 1 pound (455 g) mushrooms, coarsely chopped
- 206 500 Low-Glycemic-Index Recipes
- 2 tablespoons (30 ml) dry vermouth
- 10 ounces (280 g) frozen chopped spinach, thawed and squeezed dry
- 2 tablespoons (10 g) grated Parmesan cheese
- 2 tablespoons (14 g) plain bread crumbs
- 1 teaspoon thyme
- 1/4 teaspoon black pepper
- 1/4 teaspoon salt
- Tenderloin
- 2 teaspoons (2.8 g) thyme
- 1 teaspoon salt
- 1 teaspoon black pepper
- 41/2 pounds (2 kg) whole beef tenderloin

57

- 3 tablespoons (42 g) butter (or margarine)
- 1/4 cup (30 g) bread crumbs
- 2 tablespoons (30 ml) vermouth
- 1 can (13 ounces or 364 g) chicken broth
- 1/2 pound (225 g) mushrooms, sliced
- 2 tablespoons (16 g) flour

Directions:

1. For the stuffing (prepare it first and set it aside): In a 12-inch (30 cm) skillet, heat butter over medium-high heat and add mushrooms.
2. Cook until golden and liquid evaporates, 12 to 15 minutes. Stir in vermouth and cook another minute. Remove skillet from heat and stir in the spinach, cheese, bread crumbs, and spices.
3. For the tenderloin: Preheat oven to 425°F (220°C, gas mark 7).
4. In a cup, mix the thyme, salt, and pepper and rub evenly over the tenderloin.
5. With a sharp knife, cut a 11h-inch-deep (3 112 cm deep) slit in the tenderloin 2 inches (5 cm) from each end.

6. Spoon the stuffing mixture into the slit and tie the tenderloin closed using cooking twine at 2-inch (5-cm) intervals.

7. Roast for 30 minutes.

8. Meanwhile in a small saucepan, melt 1 tablespoon (14 g) butter over low heat and then remove pan from heat and stir in the bread crumbs.

9. Sprinkle the bread crumb mixture over the tenderloin and roast 10 to 15 minutes longer or until internal temperature reaches 145°F (63°C) for medium-rare.

10. Transfer to a platter and let rest. While resting, prepare the mushroom gravy.

11. Add vermouth and 112 cup (120 ml) chicken broth to the roasting pan and stir over low heat until the browned bits are loosened. Skim off the fat and add the remaining chicken broth.

12. In a separate pan, heat remaining butter over medium-high heat, add mushrooms, and cook until golden and liquid evaporates, about 12 minutes.

13. Stir in flour. Gradually stir in the meat juice mixture and cook, stirring constantly, until the gravy boils and thickens slightly.
14. To serve: Remove cooking twine, cut tenderloin into slices, and garnish with thyme sprigs

Nutritional Info:231 g water; 808 calories (70% from fat, 27% from protein, 3% from carb); 54 g protein; 62 g total fat; 26 g

27. Rib-Eye Steak With Wine Sauce

YIELD: 4 servings

Ingredients:

- 1 1/2 pounds (680 g) rib-eye steak 1 tablespoon olive oil
- 2 shallots
- 1/2 cup dry red wine
- 1/2 cup beef stock, or 1/2 teaspoon beef bouillon concentrate dissolved in 1/2 cup water

- 1 tablespoon balsamic vinegar
- 1 tablespoon dried thyme
- 1 teaspoon brown or Dijon mustard
- 3 tablespoons butter
- Salt and ground black pepper, to taste

Directions:

1. Cook your steak in the olive oil as described in Pan-Broiled Steak
2. In the meantime, assemble everything for your wine sauce—chop your shallots and combine the wine, beef stock, vinegar, thyme, and mustard in a measuring cup with a pouring lip.
3. Whisk them together.
4. When the timer goes off, flip the steak and set the timer again.
5. When your steak is done, put it on a platter and set it in a warm place.
6. Pour the wine mixture into the skillet and stir it around, scraping up the nice brown bits, and let it boil hard.

7. Continue boiling your sauce until it's reduced by at least half.

8. Melt in the butter, season with salt and pepper, and serve with your steak.

Nutritional Info: Calories; 28 g fat; 35 g protein; 2 g carbohydrate;

28. Beef, Bean, and Cabbage Stew

Yield: 5 servings

Ingredients:

- 1 pound lean ground beef
- ½ cup chopped onion
- 1 cup cole slaw mix or shredded cabbage
- 2 cups canned no-salt-added canned tomatoes
- 2 cups (342 g) cooked Mexican beans
- 1 cup water

Directions:

1. Break beef up into fine pieces and brown with the chopped onion and slaw mix or cabbage until the vegetables become clear.
2. Add tomatoes, beans, and water.
3. Bring to boil and simmer 10 minutes to blend the flavors.

Nutritional Info: 265 g water; 345 calories (39% from fat, 35% from protein, 25% from carb); 30 g protein; 15 g total fat; 6 g

29.   Mexican Beef Salad

Yield: 4 servings

Ingredients:

- 1 pound ground beef, extra lean
- ½ cup chopped onion
- 1 tablespoon chili powder
- 2 teaspoons oregano
- ½ teaspoon cumin
- 1 cup cooked kidney beans, drained and rinsed
- 1 pound chickpeas, drained and rinsed
- 1 cup diced tomato
- 2 cups iceberg lettuce
- ½ cup shredded Cheddar cheese

Directions:

1. Cook ground beef and onion in a skillet over medium-high heat until beef is no longer pink, 10 to 12 minutes.
2. Drain. Stir in chili powder, oregano, and cumin.
3. Cook for 1 minute.

4. Mix in beans, chickpeas, and tomato.

5. Portion lettuce onto serving plates. Top with shredded cheese.

6. Then top with beef mixture.

Nutritional Info: 263 g water; 601 calories (42% from fat, 27% from protein, 31% from carb); 41 g protein; 28 g total fat; 12 g

30. Griddled Steak Chunks with Rice

Serves 4 prep 10 mins cook 30 mins

Ingredients:

- 2 tbsp olive oil

- 1 red onion, finely chopped
- salt and freshly ground black pepper
- 2 cloves garlic, finely chopped
- 8oz basmati rice
- 2 pints vegetable stock
- 4½oz frozen peas
- handful of flat-leaf parsley,
- finely chopped
- handful of fresh mint,
- finely chopped
- handful of fresh cilantro,
- finely chopped
- 1lb 2oz (500g) lean steak

Directions:

1. Heat 1 tablespoon of the oil in a large frying pan and add half the onion.
2. Cook over low heat for 5 minutes or until soft.
3. Season with salt and pepper, then stir in the garlic.

4. Add the rice and stir to coat with the oil.

5. Pour in a little of the stock and let it bubble, add a little more, and stir again.

6. Gradually add the rest of the stock as it is absorbed and cook for 15 minutes until the rice is soft and tender, then stir in the peas.

7. Heat through for 1–2 minutes, then remove from the heat and stir in the herbs.

8. Cover with a lid and set aside.

9. Coat the steak with the remaining olive oil and season. Heat a griddle pan until hot, then add the steak and grill for 3–5 minutes each side or until cooked to your liking.

10. Remove and let rest for a few minutes, then slice and

11. arrange over the rice. Sprinkle over the remaining onion and serve.

Nutritional Info: 488cals/2,039kJ Carbohydrate 52g Sugar 2.5g Fiber 2g Fat 13g Saturated fat 3.5g Sodium 0.52g

31. Shepherd's Pie

Serves 6

Ingredients:

- 1 medium head cauliflower, chopped into 2-inch florets
- 1 pound parsnips, chopped into 2-inch pieces
- ½ cup skim milk
- 3 tablespoons low-fat cream cheese
- Salt and freshly ground black pepper
- 1 pound lean ground beef
- 2 tablespoons olive oil, divided
- 1 pound mushrooms, sliced
- 3 carrots, chopped
- 3 stalks celery, chopped
- 1 leek, chopped
- 3 garlic cloves, minced
- 1 cup low-sodium chicken broth
- ½ cup green lentils
- 3 tablespoons chopped fresh thyme leaves
- 1 tablespoon chopped fresh rosemary
- 1 bay leaf
- 1 teaspoon Worcestershire sauce
- ½ teaspoon ground cumin
- 2 tablespoons all-purpose flour

71

Directions:

1. Preheat the oven to 425°F.
2. Arrange the cauliflower and parsnips on a baking sheet, spray lightly with olive oil, and roast until they begin to brown, about 25 minutes.
3. Immediately transfer the vegetables to a blender or food processor, along with the milk and cream cheese; season to taste with salt and pepper.
4. Puree until smooth and set aside.
5. Reduce the oven temperature to 350°F.
6. Meanwhile, cook the beef, stirring occasionally, in a medium-size pan over medium heat until browned, about 5–6 minutes.
7. Transfer the beef to a bowl.
8. Using the same pan, heat 1 tablespoon olive oil over medium-high heat.
9. Add the mushrooms and cook, stirring occasionally, until browned, 4–5 minutes.
10. Transfer to the bowl with the beef.
11. Using the same pan, heat the remaining 1 tablespoon olive oil over medium heat.
12. Add the carrots, celery, leek, and garlic and cook, stirring occasionally, for 3 minutes.
13. Add the chicken broth, lentils, thyme, rosemary, bay leaf, Worcestershire sauce, and cumin.
14. Cover, reduce the heat, and simmer for about10 minutes.

15. Stir in the flour and cook, uncovered, until it begins to thicken and the lentils are al dente, about 5 minutes.
16. Discard the bay leaf and then pour the lentil mixture into the bowl with the beef and mushrooms and stir well to combine.
17. Spread the beef-lentil mixture evenly in a 9 × 13–inch baking dish.
18. Spread the mashed cauliflower mixture evenly on top.
19. Bake the shepherd's pie until piping hot and golden brown on top, about 20 minutes.

Nutrition Information: Calories: 310 Calories from Fat: 70 Total Fat: 7 grams Saturated Fat: 2 grams

32. Beef Casserole with Herby Dumplings

Serves 4

Ingredients:

- 1 lb lean braising steak, fat removed and cubed
- 8 oz swede, peeled and diced
- 8 oz baby onions or shallots, peeled
- 5 oz button mushrooms, halved
- 2 large carrots, sliced
- 2 bouquet garni
  - boiling beef stock
- 1 tbsp Worcestershire sauce

For the dumplings

- 3 oz self-raising flour
- oz shredded suet
- tsp dried mixed herbs
- salt and freshly ground black pepper

Directions:

1. Place the braising steak, vegetables, bouquet garni, stock and Worcestershire sauce in a large ovenproof casserole dish.
2. Season to taste. Bring to the boil on the hob.
3. Cover and transfer to a preheated oven at 180°C (350°F) Gas Mark 4 for 1 hour, stirring occasionally.
4. Mix together all the ingredients for the dumplings in a small bowl.
5. Add enough water to form a soft elastic dough. With floured hands, form 8 balls.
6. Add to the casserole after 1 hour of cooking.
7. Cook for a further 1 hour stirring occasionally.
8. Remove the bouquet garni before serving.
9. Serve with a jacket potato and freshly cooked vegetables.

Nutritional Info: calories 579, 16 g fat 52g protein 60g carbohydrate

33.   Easy Beef Enchiladas

Servings 10 enchiladas

Ingredients:

- pound ground sirloin
- teaspoons chili powder
- 1 cup salsa
- 1 cup corn
- 1 cup packed fresh baby spinach
- 1 1/2 cups shredded reduced-fat Mexican blend cheese
- 10 flour tortillas room temperature, 6–8-inch
- 1 1/2 cups enchilada sauce found in can
- 1 bunch green onions chopped

Directions:

1. Preheat oven 350°F. Coat 13 x 9 x 2-inch baking dish with nonstick cooking spray.
2. In large nonstick skillet, cook meat 6–8 minutes or until meat is done and drain any excess fat.
3. Add chili powder, salsa, corn, and spinach; continue cooking about 5 minutes.
4. Remove from heat, set aside.
5. Spoon about 1/4 cup meat mixture and 1 tablespoon cheese onto a tortilla.
6. Roll and place seam side down in prepared baking dish.

7. Repeat with remaining tortillas.
8. Pour enchilada sauce evenly over filled tortillas in baking dish and sprinkle with any remaining cheese and green onions.
9. Bake, covered with foil for 20 minutes or until thoroughly heated.

Nutritional Info: Per Serving: Calories 237, Calories from Fat 24%, Fat 6g, Saturated Fat 3g, Cholesterol 35mg, Sodium 739mg, Carbohydrates 28g

34.   Tasty Beef Curry

Serves: 4

Ingredients:

- tbsp sunflower oil
- 1 large onion, thinly sliced
- 5½ oz button mushrooms, sliced

- 14 oz sirloin steak, trimmed of fat and cut into thin strips
- 1½ tsp bottled chopped root ginger in oil, drained
- garlic cloves, crushed
- ½ tsp crushed dried chillies
- tsp ground coriander
- ¼ tsp ground cardamom
- ½ tsp turmeric
- ¼ tsp grated nutmeg
- 1 can chopped tomatoes, about 400 g
- 1 tsp cornflour mixed with 1 tbsp water
- 300 g (10½ oz) plain low-fat yogurt
- 1 tbsp clear honey
- 4½ oz young spinach leaves
- juice of ½ lime
- 2 tbsp chopped fresh coriander, plus extra leaves to garnish
- Cardamom rice
- 12 oz basmati rice, well rinsed
- 1 cinnamon stick
- 8 whole green cardamom pods, cracked
- juice of ½ lemon
- salt

Directions:

1. Heat the oil in a large saucepan and add the onion and mushrooms.
2. Cook over a high heat for 2 minutes or until the onion slices begin to colour.
3. Add the beef together with the ginger, garlic, chillies, ground coriander, cardamom, turmeric and nutmeg. Cook for 2 minutes, stirring well, then add the omatoes with their juice and the cornflour mixture.
4. Bring to the boil, stirring.
5. Stir in the yogurt and honey.
6. Bring back to the boil, then reduce the heat, cover and simmer gently for 20 minutes.
7. Meanwhile, prepare the cardamom rice.
8. Put 450 ml (15 fl oz) cold water in a saucepan and bring to the boil.
9. Add the rice, cinnamon stick and cardamom pods. Bring back to the boil, then cover tightly and cook for 10 minutes or until the rice is tender.
10. Drain and return the rice to the saucepan.
11. Stir in the lemon juice and keep covered until the curry is ready to serve.
12. Stir the spinach, lime juice and chopped coriander into the curry and allow the leaves to wilt down into the sauce.
13. To serve, spoon the curry over the rice and garnish with fresh coriander leaves.

35.   Beef and vegetable casserole

Serves: 4

Ingredients:

Ingredients

- 900g (2 lb) beef rump steak, cut into chunks
- 2 large onions, sliced
- 2 tablespoons plain flour
- salt and pepper to taste
- 3 tablespoons olive oil
- 600ml(1 pint) beef stock
- 6 med-large potatoes, quartered

Directions:

1. Preheat the oven to 175 degrees C
2. Place the flour, onions and beef into a large resealable food bag.
3. Add salt and pepper , seal bag and shake well so all of the meat and onions are lightly covered in flour.
4. Heat the olive oil in a large frying pan over medium-high heat, and then add the contents of the bag into the pan to sear the meat.
5. Next, pour in all of the beef stock and let simmer gently for a few minutes.

6. Pour contents of the frying pan into a casserole dish.
7. Place the potatoes in the casserole dish so half of the potato quarter is above the surface, half below.
8. Bake in a preheated oven for 2 hours, or until meat is tender and the potatoes are cooked through.

36.   Ropa Vieja

Serving: 6

Ingredients

- beef flank steak (2 pounds)
- 1/2 teaspoon salt
- 1/2 teaspoon pepper
- cups beef broth
- 1/2 cup dry vermouth
- 1/2 cup dry red wine or additional beef broth
- 1 can (6 ounces) tomato paste
- 1 large onion, thinly sliced
- 1 large carrot, sliced
- 1 small sweet red pepper, thinly sliced
- 1 Cubanelle or mild banana pepper, thinly sliced
- springs fresh oregano
- Hot cooked rice

Directions:

1. Cut steak into 6 pieces; sprinkle with salt and pepper.
2. Heat a large skillet over medium-high heat; brown meat in batches.
3. Transfer meat to a 5- or 6-qt. slow cooker.
4. Add broth, vermouth, wine and tomato paste to pan.

5. Cook 2-3 minutes, stirring to loosen browned bits from pan. Pour over meat.
6. Top with onion, carrot, red pepper, Cubanelle pepper and oregano.
7. Cook, covered, on low until meat is tender, 8-10 hours. Remove oregano sprigs; discard.
8. Remove meat; shred with 2 forks.
9. Return to slow cooker; heat through.
10.   Serve with rice and, if desired, additional oregano, lime wedges and green olives.

Nutrition Facts:

1 serving: 278 calories, 11g fat (5g saturated fat), 72mg cholesterol, 611mg sodium, 10g carbohydrate (5g sugars, 2g fiber), 32g protein.

37.   Cabbage Bean Stew

Serving: 6

Ingredients

- 1/2 pound lean ground beef (90% lean)
- 3 cups shredded cabbage or angel hair coleslaw mix
- can (16 ounces) red beans, rinsed and drained
- 1 can (14-1/2 ounces) diced tomatoes, undrained
- 1 can (8 ounces) tomato sauce
- 3/4 cup salsa or picante sauce
- 1 medium green pepper, chopped
- 1 small onion, chopped
- garlic cloves, minced

- 1 teaspoon ground cumin
- 1/2 teaspoon pepper
- Shredded cheddar cheese and sliced jalapeno peppers, optional

Directions:

1. In a large skillet, cook beef over medium heat 4-6 minutes or until no longer pink, breaking into crumbles; drain.
2. Transfer meat to a 4-qt. slow cooker.
3. Stir in remaining ingredients.
4. Cook, covered, on low 6-8 hours or until cabbage is tender.
5. If desired, top with shredded cheddar cheese and sliced jalapeno peppers.

Nutrition Facts

1 cup: 177 calories, 4g fat (1g saturated fat), 24mg cholesterol, 591mg sodium, 23g carbohydrate (5g sugars, 7g fiber), 13g protein

38. Mushroom Meat Loaf

Serving: 6

Ingredients

- large egg, lightly beaten
- 1/4 pound fresh mushrooms, chopped
- 1/2 cup old-fashioned oats
- 1/2 cup chopped red onion
- 1/4 cup ground flaxseed
- 1/2 teaspoon pepper
- 1 package (19-1/2 ounces) Italian turkey sausage links, casings removed, crumbled
- 1 pound lean ground beef (90% lean)
- 1 cup marinara or spaghetti sauce
- Shredded Parmesan cheese, optional

Directions

1. Preheat oven to 350°.
2. In a large bowl, combine the egg, mushrooms, oats, onion, flax and pepper.
3. Crumble turkey and beef over mixture; mix lightly but thoroughly.
4. Shape into a 10x4-in. loaf.
5. Place in a 13x9-in. baking dish coated with cooking spray.
6. Bake, uncovered, for 50 minutes; drain.
7. Top with marinara sauce.

8. Bake until no pink remains and a thermometer reads 165°, 10-15 minutes longer.
9. If desired, top with Parmesan cheese.

Nutrition Facts

1 slice: 261 calories, 14g fat (3g saturated fat), 103mg cholesterol, 509mg sodium, 10g carbohydrate (3g sugars, 2g fiber), 25g protein.

39. Teriyaki Beef Stew

Serving: 6

Ingredients

- 2 pounds beef stew meat
- bottle (12 ounces) ginger beer or ginger ale
- 1/4 cup teriyaki sauce
- garlic cloves, minced

- tablespoons sesame seeds
- 2 tablespoons cornstarch
- 2 tablespoons cold water
- 2 cups frozen peas, thawed
- Hot cooked rice, optional

Directions

1. In a large nonstick skillet, brown beef in batches. Transfer to a 3-qt. slow cooker.
2. In a small bowl, combine the ginger beer, teriyaki sauce, garlic and sesame seeds; pour over beef.
3. Cover and cook on low for 6-8 hours, until meat is tender.
4. Combine cornstarch and cold water until smooth; gradually stir into stew.
5. Stir in peas. Cover and cook on high for 30 minutes or until thickened.
6. Serve with rice if desired.

Nutrition Facts

1 cup stew: 310 calories, 12g fat (4g saturated fat), 94mg cholesterol, 528mg sodium, 17g carbohydrate (9g sugars, 2g fiber), 33g protein.

40.   Mexican Meat Loaf

Serving: 8

Ingredients

- 6 tablespoons ketchup, divided
- 2 tablespoons Worcestershire sauce
- 12 saltines, crushed
- medium onion, finely chopped
- 6 garlic cloves, minced
- 1 teaspoon paprika
- 1/2 teaspoon salt
- 1/2 teaspoon pepper
- 1/8 teaspoon cayenne pepper
- pounds lean ground beef

Directions:

1. Cut three 20x3-in. strips of heavy-duty foil; crisscross so they resemble spokes of a wheel.
2. Place strips on the bottom and up the sides of a 3-qt. slow cooker.
3. Coat strips with cooking spray.
4. In a large bowl, combine 2 tablespoons ketchup, Worcestershire sauce, saltines, onion, garlic, paprika, salt, pepper and cayenne.
5. Crumble beef over mixture and mix well.
6. Shape into a round loaf. Place in the center of the strips. Cover and cook on low until no pink

remains and a thermometer reads 160°, 4-5 hours.

7. Using foil strips as handles, remove the meat loaf to a platter.

8. Spread remaining ketchup over top.

Nutrition Facts

1 slice: 222 calories, 10g fat (4g saturated fat), 71mg cholesterol, 447mg sodium, 10g carbohydrate (5g sugars, 1g fiber), 23g protein